Personal Achievement Log (PAL)

10 Days to Maximum Teaching Success

Annette L. Breaux

EYE ON EDUCATION
6 DEPOT WAY WEST, SUITE 106
LARCHMONT, NY 10538
(914) 833–0551
(914) 833–0761 fax
www.eyeoneducation.com

10 9 8 7 6 5 4 3

Editorial and production services provided by
Richard H. Adin, Freelance Editorial Services
52 Oakwood Blvd., Poughkeepsie, NY 12603-4112
(914-471-3566)

Table of Contents

Day 1

Conditioning Yourself for Maximum Teaching Success

CD 1 Track 1

Key Points

- What this training will do is help you to condition yourself for maximum success in the classroom—every single day that you teach. Every day, for 10 days, you will listen to one CD for about twenty minutes. Then you'll have an assignment, based on what we've discussed in the session, that you can actually put into practice the very next day. You'll see the results **tomorrow** —and you'll keep track of your progress here, in your Personal Achievement Log. Notice that the acronym for Personal Achievement Log is PAL, which is fitting, because this log will become your best pal for the next 10 days, and hopefully for a lot longer than that.

- At the end of the 10 days, you'll be absolutely amazed at your progress and your growth as a teacher.

- Are your students 1' s, 2' s, or 3' s?

  1's—One's do the wrong thing, even if they're being watched.

  2's—Two's do the right thing, but only if they're being watched.

  3's—Three's do the right thing even if they're **not** being watched.

- Ultimately, we, as teachers, try to train all of our students to be 3's. Therefore, we, as teachers and role models, have got to be 3's.

Characteristics of 3's as teachers:

- You walk out of their rooms and say "Wow!" You can just sense their effectiveness.

- You listen to their discussions with others—anywhere—and know that they love teaching and are good at it. They always "appear" happy! Now is anyone always happy? Of course not. But the 3's know that as professionals, it's important to appear happy and in control when you're on the job.

- 3's don't care when you come in to observe them—they're always teaching!

- They are the teachers the students **love**, and the ones who can get the most challenging kids to do almost anything.

- These are the teachers who touch lives and make a difference.

- These are the teachers who do not engage in "school gossip," because they know that no matter how tempting it may be, it goes against everything we stand for as teachers and as professionals.
- These are the teachers who embrace change. No matter how difficult it may be, they're always willing to give it their best shot!
- Just because they're 3's does not mean they have special talents or know all of the answers, but rather it means that they're always in pursuit of becoming more effective.

Activity

Think back to your former teachers...

List 5 characteristics of your all-time favorite teacher.

_____

_____

_____

_____

_____

List 5 characteristics of your **least** favorite teacher.

_____

_____

_____

_____

_____

A very interesting point is the fact that no one ever mentions how many degrees their favorite teachers had or how many years of experience their favorite teachers had—nor do they ever list all of the "content" they learned in the classrooms of these teachers. Instead, the characteristics always seem to reflect what kind of person the teacher was and how that teacher made the students feel about themselves…

List 5 characteristics that **you would like your students to list about you** if they were to remember you as their favorite teacher.

_____

_____

_____

_____

_____

Assignment

Part 1

Refer to your PAL list containing the five characteristics that you would like your students to remember about you. Choose one of those characteristics start working on it tomorrow. Assume that one of your characteristics is that you want students to remember that you cared about each of them. Tomorrow you may decide to demonstrate extra caring and extra patience. You might even tell your students what a joy it is to teach them and that you really do care about all of them and their future successes. And then, of course, continue to express that sense of caring every day that you teach. You'll be amazed at the results!

Please record your results here for part one of your assignment.

_____

_____

_____

_____

_____

_____

_____

Part 2

Your second assignment is to explain to your students that there are three kinds of students—1's, 2's, and 3's. Elaborate on what each means, and ask your students to determine, without sharing with anyone, of course, whether they are 1's, 2's, or 3's. (Don't forget to give them the benefit of the doubt by stating that you know they are at least 2's.) And then tell them that you are committed to helping each of them, before the end of the school year, to become 3's.

That's it! Do those two simple assignments, and see your teaching and your students' learning improve tomorrow!

Please record your results here for part two of your assignment.

_____

_____

_____

_____

_____

_____

_____

_____

_____

_____

_____

_____

_____

_____

I Teach

I light a spark in a darkened soul
I warm the heart of one grown cold
I look beyond and see within
Behind the face, beneath the skin
I quench a thirst, I soothe a pain
I provide the food that will sustain
I touch, I love, I laugh, I cry
Whatever is needed, I supply
Yet more than I give, I gain from each
I am most richly blessed—I teach.

Annette L. Breaux

Day 2

Establishing Excellent Classroom Management

CD 1 Track 2

Key Points

- The lack of well-rehearsed **procedures** is what causes most discipline problems.

- **Classroom management involves all that you do as a teacher to make your classroom run smoothly**—from how you arrange the furniture to how well you plan your lessons to how you deal with students on a consistent basis to how well-rehearsed and consistently implemented your procedures and routines are to how consistent you are with your discipline plan, etc.

- **A procedure is a consistent way of doing something.** In the classroom, procedures are needed for things such as entering the room, asking permission to speak, walking to and from lunch, passing in papers, etc.

- Difference between rules and procedures: Rules have consequences and procedures do not.

- **Fact**

    If you tell a student what you want, show him exactly how to do it, practice with him how to do it, and praise him when he succeeds, then the chances of his actually doing it increase a hundredfold!

- If you want to be a good teacher, you have to be a good classroom manager. **How do you ensure effective classroom management?** By establishing consistent routines and procedures so that students know exactly what is expected of them and how they should do certain things in your classroom.

- **How to establish a procedure:** Tell students about the procedure, show them how to do it, practice it with them until they get it right, and remind them and practice again and again as often as necessary.

Activity

Write **one word** that would describe what you would witness in a classroom where there is no classroom management: _____

List as many things as you can that would **require a procedure** in the classroom.

_____

_____

_____

_____

_____

_____

_____

Assignment

Go into your classroom tomorrow and implement **one new procedure.** Then, practice it consistently. Please record your results here.

_____

_____

_____

_____

_____

_____

An Ounce of Inspiration

Give me an ounce of inspiration

Leading, of course, to motivation

Which will spark my imagination

Thus, you'll see my perspiration

As I feel my mind's vibration

Spurring on my new creation

Concentration for the duration

Whew! I did it! Pure elation!

Annette L. Breaux

Day 3

Handling Discipline Challenges Effectively

CD 1 Track 3

Key Points

- **People appreciate and respond to environments where they are made to feel appreciated and special.** Therefore, it is important to stand at your classroom door every day and every class period in order to enthusiastically greet your students as they enter your classroom.
- Students like to be where they feel welcomed, and students succeed and behave in positive environments.
- **The better the classroom is managed, the fewer the discipline problems.** Having consistently enforced—clear routines and procedures will reduce discipline problems drastically!
- **Even the most effective teachers deal with issues involving discipline.** As long as there are students, there will be discipline challenges. Whether those "challenges" escalate into full-blown problems hinges greatly upon how *we*, as teachers, deal with the challenges.
- **Effective teachers do two things:** They treat every student with respect and dignity, and they know how to defuse potential discipline problems.

Bag of Tricks:

- Use good psychology with students to deter discipline problems.
- Use the "Are you all right?" technique with students.
- Be proactive—not reactive—in dealing with issues of discipline.
- Avoid "down time" in the classroom.
- Teach every day from bell to bell!
- Try timing your students during transitions.
- Adhere to the "Faculty Meeting Rule"—Don't do anything to a student in your classroom that you would not feel comfortable having done to you by your principal in a faculty meeting.

Assignment

Part 1

Tomorrow, greet your students enthusiastically at the classroom door. If you already greet them daily, then be a little more enthusiastic than you usually are. Then record your results and/or comments here.

_____

_____

_____

_____

_____

_____

_____

_____

_____

_____

_____

_____

_____

_____

_____

_____

_____

_____

_____

_____

_____

Part 2

Tomorrow, implement one new technique that you've learned from today's session. Record your results below.

_____

_____

_____

_____

_____

_____

_____

_____

_____

_____

_____

_____

_____

_____

_____

_____

_____

_____

_____

_____

_____

_____

A Very Clever Teacher

We had to draw a picture one day
But I couldn't decide what to draw
So I decided to leave my paper blank
And my teacher looked at it in awe
"What a beautiful fluffy white cloud" she said,
"May I hang it on the wall?"
And I realized that she did not notice
That I had drawn nothing at all
Then she proudly hung for all to see
The work I had not done
But with her permission I took it home
And I added the sky and the sun
And now that I think about it
I wonder if she really knew
That my drawing was not of a cloud at all
It was work I did not do
I thought that I had tricked her
But maybe it was she
Who used a clever way to get me to draw
A picture for all to see.

Annette L. Breaux

Day 4

Controlling Your Actions and Reactions with Students

CD 2 Track 1

Key Points

- **Effective teachers "defuse" potentially volatile situations in the classroom.** In the case of Albert Wilson, Mrs. Adams "defused" the situation and did not take Albert's behavior personally. Diane Adams could have chosen to display the same reaction to frustration as did Albert. She could have added fuel to the fire (that Albert had managed to spark) by allowing herself to be reduced to the level where emotions rule. She could have yelled at Albert, pointing out how disrespectful and rude he was being (which, of course, were his intentions to begin with). She could have ordered him out of the room, to the office, or chosen some other familiar course of action to which less effective teachers are accustomed. Thank goodness she didn't!

- **The bottom line is that**
  - ◆ It takes one person to be disrespectful, but it takes two people to turn it into a power struggle.
  - ◆ Effective teachers do not engage in power struggles. Instead, they defuse them.
  - ◆ Effective teachers do not take disrespect personally. They recognize the frustration of the student, they think through their reactions to the student, and then they act in a professional manner.
  - ◆ Once a student knows that you are "on his side" as opposed to being "out to get him," he will stop trying to get YOU!
  - ◆ And the fact is that even the "hardest" hearts can be softened with the right approach!

Activity

List **3 ways that you feel on the inside** when you feel extremely angry or frustrated and **3 ways that you "look" or "appear" on the outside** when you're in this particular state. Be honest—describe yourself in detail—3 ways that you feel on the inside and 3 ways that you appear on the outside.

_____

_____

_____

_____

_____

_____

_____

_____

_____

_____

_____

_____

_____

_____

_____

_____

_____

_____

_____

Key Points

- **As teachers, we're all human.** Of course we get angry, of course we get frustrated, of course we feel like we could just scream. But the real key is: Do you let the students know how you're feeling by your actions?

- **It's not our feelings that determine who we are to others, but rather our actions.** And one of the most difficult tasks to accomplish as a teacher is the ability to control your actions and maintain your composure at all costs. Yes, students will "try" you. They will "work on your nerves." They will "go for your jugular"—not because they're bad, but because they're children. And for a child to be able to "control" an adult's emotions is a very powerful feeling.

- An important word of advice: **Don't play the game**.

You will feel frustrated at times. That's normal. But to roll your eyes, clench your teeth when you speak, fold your arms and tap your foot as you stare at the ceiling, sigh, raise your voice, or exhibit any of the many signs of a loss of composure will only serve to let students know that you *did* play, you *did* lose, and you gave your control over to them. You can be serious without looking angry. You can discipline a child in a thoughtful, professional manner. You see, there is never an appropriate time to "lose your cool." You are a professional, and you must act as a professional at all times. Therefore, you must "never let them see you sweat." When students realize that you will not play the game and that you are truly a professional, they will stop trying to see how red they can make your face get, how far that vein in your neck will stick out... In turn, you'll earn their respect, but most importantly, you'll serve as the role model that so many of them so desperately need.

So how do you do it? How do you control your actions and reactions with your students? You just do it. You maintain your composure, just like we teach our students to learn to keep their cool when they get angry or frustrated. And if you have to, you fake it! You never let them see you sweat.

Remember that by controlling your actions and reactions in the classroom, you put your students at ease. And the fact is that **when students are at ease, they will do their best, they will accept challenges, they will behave, they will succeed, and most importantly, they will never forget you for it!**

Assignment

When you go into your classroom tomorrow, remain consciously aware of every single time you feel frustrated or aggravated with a student. Don't worry—it will happen, unless your students don't show up tomorrow. And every time it happens, make a conscious effort *not* to let it show. In other words, go into your classroom tomorrow and practice "faking" it. Do whatever it takes *not* to let your students know when they get to you. Then write about the experience here. Think about how you felt, and what you did differently than what you would typically do. And then record your results.

_____

_____

_____

_____

_____

_____

_____

_____

_____

_____

_____

_____

_____

_____

_____

Lost Within a Shout

You yelled at me and I yelled back

What else was there to do?

We yelled some more, our throats got sore

And the tension grew and grew

And finally, in exhaustion, we both ran out of steam

Left standing in embarrassment, no pride left to
redeem

What point is there in thinking that being "right" we
must

And pushing on till all involved just lose respect and
trust?

Maybe if we'd listened, we could have met half way

Let's talk next time and really hear what the other has
to say

For if we both could do that, maybe we'd find out

That never has a point been made when lost within a
shout!

Annette L. Breaux

Planning
Effective Lessons

CD 2 Track 2

Activity

Please write everything you've noticed about the structure of this training thus far from day one.

_____

_____

_____

_____

_____

_____

_____

_____

_____

_____

_____

_____

_____

_____

_____

_____

_____

_____

_____

_____

_____

_____

_____

How the Training Has Been Structured

- The training is highly structured and very fast paced.
- My approach in working with you is one of respect, and I truly BELIEVE that you can and will succeed with this training.
- I'm enthusiastic in my teaching—as all teachers should be.
- Each day's lesson intentionally builds upon the previous day's lesson.
- The lessons are short, motivational, and full of energy, and each day's assignments are small, yet meaningful.
- The training is structured in small bites—one activity, one success at a time.

You see, I know something: I know that if I leave a bad taste in your mouth, you won't come back. And I want for you to come back every day—because that's the only way this training can truly work for you. So I plan each lesson just as if I were teaching lessons in the classroom—paying special attention to the fact that each lesson is inviting, informative, not overwhelming, fun, humorous, and doable.

If we could plan every one of our lessons for our students like that every day, our students would truly amaze us—and we would literally amaze ourselves.

Key Points

- When you plan lessons, **plan in "small bites"**—small segments that last no longer than 10 or 15 minutes. For 15 minutes, plan to teach a skill, get the students really excited, and then get them busy doing something so that they can experience immediate success. All of these segments are simply parts of one bigger lesson for the day—but make sure that you're moving quickly from one activity to the next, make sure that you're getting your students excited with your own enthusiasm, make sure that everything you give them to do is doable—and then move on.

- **Variety is key**—and that takes effective planning on your part. If each segment of your lesson is fun, inviting, exciting, and doable, you've got a recipe for student success every time. So if you've got a 90-minute block, you can plan 6 different segments—six different types of activities that all focus on your main objective for the day. This way, it's so highly structured that the students never have time to get bored or restless.

- As the saying goes—if you're failing to plan, you're planning to fail. It's that simple. And don't ever think that your students will not know if you're "winging it." They see it, they sense it, and they respond to the lack of structure accordingly! The fact is that planning does take time, skill, and thought, but when you plan well, then most of your work is done. Now you can go and have fun teaching the lesson. Teachers who do not plan good lessons end up struggling with behavior problems, off-task students, and general chaos, not to mention that in order for the students to learn a new skill, the lesson must be well thought out and well taught.

- Remember, surgeons go into surgery with highly structured plans—thank goodness. Coaches go into games with very specific game plans, and attorneys appear in court to defend their clients with highly detailed plans. We would expect no less of them, and thus, in teaching children, we should expect no less of ourselves.

- **Make your objectives clear to your students for every lesson that you teach.**

Simply stated, an objective defines what the students should know or be able to do at the end of each lesson. I've often watched teachers tell students to read a chapter and answer the questions at the end of the chapter when they're finished. The students reluctantly get busy, but they have no idea "why" they have to do this. In fact, it's a good rule to remember that when students ask, "Why do we have to do this?" it's like a red flag reminding you that you have obviously forgotten to make the objective for the lesson clear. It goes without saying that you, the teacher, must write clear, measurable objectives for every lesson you teach. But that's not enough. You must now make those objectives clear to your students. Make it a point, as you begin each lesson, to tell your students, "Guess what you'll be able to do at the end of this lesson," and then tell them. That way, you'll know where you're going, students will know what they're learning, and you'll all arrive at your destination safely.

A Simple Checklist for Planning

Every time you sit down to plan a lesson, think about the following:

☐ Is my objective clear and measurable and does it come from my district's curriculum?

☐ Is my entire lesson student-oriented, relating to real life and actively involving the students?

☐ Do all of my activities focus on accomplishing the lesson's objective?

☐ Does my lesson include the basic parts of any effective lesson: some type of introduction where I grab students' attention and relate the new skill to real life learning, then an activity where I actually teach and model the new skill followed by an activity where the students and I practice the new skill together, followed by an activity where the students practice the new skill independently, followed by a review activity to provide closure?

☐ And throughout my lesson, do I have ways of determining whether my students are understanding the concept?

Assignment

Using the checklist I shared with you, look at one of tomorrow's lesson plans. Check off everything you already have in place. And then add whatever's left to your lesson. After you teach the lesson, record your results here.

_____

_____

_____

_____

_____

_____

_____

_____

_____

_____

_____

_____

_____

_____

_____

_____

_____

_____

_____

_____

_____

I'll Do it Tomorrow

I didn't feel like doing it, so I put it off for a day

And the next day came and I put off more—too much
was coming my way

I used up tons of paper with my list of "things to do"

And every day my "list of things" just grew and grew
and grew

It overtook my kitchen, then overtook my house

It overtook my children and it overtook my spouse

If only I had done the things that needed to be done

It would have been much easier to do things one by
one

But now I'm overwhelmed with all the things I did not
do

How will I survive this? I do not have a clue!

And sitting atop these things to do are feelings of guilt
and sorrow

So I'm turning over a new leaf. Yep, I'll do it tomorrow!

Annette L. Breaux

Utilizing Teaching Strategies That Work

CD 2 Track 3

Key Points

- Our students will never be perfect, and neither will we. We continue to learn new and better ways of teaching, and lots of times we learn what works by figuring out, through our own mistakes, what doesn't work.

- It's a good thing to continue to make mistakes so that we can capitalize on the opportunities to learn from our mistakes. So please allow yourselves to continue *not* to be perfect.

- It's just like medicine—teaching is not an exact science, but we continue to learn new and innovative ways of doing things so that our students can reap the benefits.

Activity

In your own words, define "real life teaching."

_____

_____

_____

_____

_____

_____

_____

_____

_____

_____

_____

_____

Key Points

- Real life teaching does mean relating the skills we teach to real life. The problem, however, lies in the term *real life*—whose real life, ours or our students?—our students, of course. But sometimes, as teachers, we forget that just because a skill is eventually important in life when you're an adult, that does not make it important to the life of a student today. We need to relate every skill we teach to the real lives of our students, not our own.

- We need to begin teaching all the skills inside the classroom just like the skills we teach outside the classroom. For example, we don't teach students to swim by having them memorize the chapter on swimming or by giving them 20 swimming vocabulary words, or by answering the questions at the end of the "swimming" chapter or by completing swimming worksheets. Children learn to swim by "doing." And that's how they should be learning in the classroom—by actually "swimming around" in the content.

- In your classroom, do you ever hear a student ask, "Why do we have to know this?" If you do, then it's a *red flag* to you that you have not made that critical "real life" connection!

- Aristotle said, "All knowledge is relational." In other words, in order for us to learn anything new, we must have something we already "know" with which to connect the new skill. When work "makes sense" to us, we have a purpose for doing it. If it does not seem meaningful, we close our minds to it. After all, what's the point in learning something that has no meaning in our lives?

Assignment

Take one of your objectives for tomorrow and make an extra effort to make a real life connection for your students. After you teach the lesson, record your results here.

_____

_____

_____

_____

_____

_____

_____

_____

_____

_____

_____

_____

_____

_____

_____

_____

_____

_____

_____

_____

Make it REAL

I just don't see the point in why I need to know this
  junk

You say if I don't learn it, then surely I will flunk

But I need a better reason for learning all this stuff

It's boring and it's pointless, so learning it is rough

And every time I'm bored in school, I think of other
  things

Lost inside a daydream, until the school bell rings

Which means I haven't learned it, which means my
  grades are bad

Which means that I'm in trouble and my mom and
  dad are mad.

And then I get so far behind that it's just too late to
  pass

So next year here I am again, I'm right back in your
  class

I didn't get it last year. I don't get it today

Please teacher, make it real to me, so that I can move
  on in May!

Annette L. Breaux

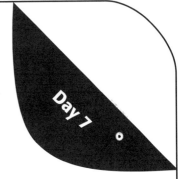
Day 7

Maintaining
the Maximum Degree
of Professionalism

CD 3 Track 1

Key Points

- Parents place their children in our classrooms and expect that we are highly qualified and that **we epitomize professionalism**—no matter what.

- We have both a need and a right to insist that **professionals, in any profession, act professionally** at all times.

- Experienced professionals cringe at the thought of having to be in the company of those who behave unprofessionally. But **true professionals remain professional** even, and especially, in the company of one behaving unprofessionally.

- By engaging in unprofessional behavior and stooping to the levels of unprofessional people, we simply add fuel to their fires and lend credence to their lack of professionalism, at least in their minds… Misery does love company, unfortunately, and people who are miserable in their job settings tend to enlist the support of others who feel the same. They are looking for justifications for their misery without having to look at themselves for answers. And every time another teacher "agrees" with what they say, their "victimization" is affirmed and the overall school environment becomes a little less professional, one teacher at a time.

- **Acting in any way other than professionally is not only ineffective, but harmful!** In acting unprofessionally, we relinquish our abilities to truly make a difference. And in enabling others to play out their roles as victims, we demoralize the profession. Dealing with difficult coworkers in a professional manner may be the ultimate test of our own professionalism.

Activity

Write the name of the most positive teacher on your faculty.

_____

Okay, now look at that name, and look at it carefully. Hopefully, you've named yourself… But the good news is that even if you didn't name yourself, you can literally become the most positive teacher on your faculty *tomorrow*. And then, hopefully, the next time you go through this training—because my hope is that you'll continue to revisit this training many more times throughout your career—hopefully next time, you'll immediately and confidently be able to name yourself.

The truth is that no teacher wants to have a negative reputation, yet many do. The best way to steer clear of a negative reputation is not to establish one in the first place, because once you have one, it's extremely difficult to change it. So teach from your heart, treat your students with dignity, carry yourself as a professional at all times, be the most enthusiastic person you know, and wear your positive reputation proudly!

Activity

List five characteristics of a true, professional teacher.

1. _____

2. _____

3. _____

4. _____

5. _____

Most teachers list things such as:

- Professional teachers are positive.
- Professional teachers treat students fairly and with dignity.
- Professional teachers do not lose their tempers with their students.
- Professional teachers do not gossip.
- Professional teachers participate willingly in initiatives to improve teaching and learning.
- Professional teachers dress like professionals, etc.

Assignment

Part One

If, by some chance, you did not name yourself as the most positive teacher in your school, begin to be that person tomorrow. And at day's end tomorrow, record here, exactly what you did to be more positive, and, if any, what changes you noticed in yourself and even in your students.

_____

_____

_____

_____

_____

_____

_____

_____

_____

_____

_____

_____

Part Two

Take your list of characteristics of teachers who are true professionals and begin to implement one of those characteristics tomorrow. Record your successes here, and then continue to implement one more characteristic a day, or, at the very least, one characteristic a week.

_____

_____

_____

_____

_____

_____

_____

_____

_____

_____

_____

_____

_____

Remember that some people go to work because they *have* to. Teachers teach because they *want* to. As any true teacher will tell you, we didn't choose teaching. Teaching chose us. We have a calling. And along with that calling comes tremendous responsibility—responsibility for touching lives and making a difference.

Now I'm Called a Professional

I took the easy road and did what I knew was wrong

But friends of mine were watching, who sang a different song

They pulled me from the doldrums—above that negative haze

They helped me come to understand the error of my ways

So I took "the road less traveled," the one that spells success

And I realized that this one, too, created quite a mess.

For those who took the easy road threw roadblocks in my way

They hate to see another win a game that they won't play

But play I did, and win I have, and now I'm called (I've heard)

"A professional," by those I trust, "in every sense of the word."

Elizabeth Breaux

Day 8

Realizing the Magnitude of Your Influence

CD 3 Track 2

Key Points

- In the words of Henry Adams, "A teacher affects eternity. He can never tell where his influence stops."
- When you become a child's teacher, you automatically become one of his greatest role models in life.

Activity

Write whatever it is that you noticed about Mrs. Johnson... What impressed you about the way she dealt with Jason? Just jot down a few thoughts about the way Mrs. Johnson treated Jason.

_____

_____

_____

_____

_____

Key points regarding the way Mrs. Johnson treated Jason:

- She never gave up on Jason—even though his behavior was unacceptable the entire school year—until the very last day.
- She never lost her cool with Jason, yet she most definitely did hold him accountable for his actions.
- Though it was probably very tempting at times, she never engaged in power struggles with Jason.
- She was intuitive enough to realize that Jason was obviously suffering terribly on the inside.
- She always found a way to make him successful.

The bottom line is that she remained a true professional throughout. Even though her frustration levels often must have been extremely high, she never revealed it to her students—and that's what true professionals do—and that's how teachers touch lives.

Key Points

As teachers, as everyday, normal, run-of-the-mill individuals, we often tend to underestimate the fact that we **truly do affect the lives of every student we teach.** This influence can be very powerful—hopefully in a positive sense—yet it can also be very harmful if we do not treat this "power" with the utmost reverence. It is often easy to say things out of frustration—things that we may think nothing of, but that students will internalize and take to heart.

The fact is that you, as a teacher, will influence the lives of every single student you teach. Whether that influence is positive or negative is completely up to you!

Whether you are a new teacher or a seasoned veteran, it's never too late to start keeping an "**I Am Special**" folder. It's a very simple concept with very special rewards. An "I Am Special" folder is simply a folder where you may keep notes from students, thank-you cards, letters of appreciation, notes to yourself about something exciting or heartwarming that happens to you on a particular day, letters from parents, etc. And on those really difficult days when you are questioning whether you truly are making a difference, just take out the folder and begin to look through it. It will reaffirm the fact that you are making a difference, it will rekindle your love of children and of teaching, and it will remind you that you have truly chosen the noblest of all professions—teaching!

Assignment

Simply get a folder and label it "I Am Special." Put at least one thing in it—maybe a letter you've received from a student or a parent—maybe your principal wrote you a nice note after observing your teaching, maybe you may want to write something about a particularly heartwarming experience you've had as a teacher, or whatever you can imagine that will help to remind you, whenever you need reminding, that you *are* special and that your influence is far greater and more profound than you will ever know.

Remember, if you impact the life of one student in a positive way, you therefore influence the person that he becomes, which will affect the life of every person he ever encounters. You will never fully realize the magnitude of your influence. But know, today and every day, that all of your actions and reactions with your students will help to determine the type of influence you will have on them—not just for today, but for the rest of their lives.

> ### *If I Could Teach My Students*
>
> If I could teach my students one solitary thing
>
> A sense of ever questioning to each one I would bring
>
> And by their curiosity, they'd learn to teach themselves
>
> For the more that one uncovers, the deeper that he delves
>
> If as one student's teacher, I light a fire within
>
> Then I have touched the world indeed—influence does not end.
>
> *Annette L. Breaux*

Defining the Teacher You Want to Be

CD 3 Track 3

Key Points

- If you want to get somewhere, you simply **map out a plan** as to where it is you want to go. And then you head in that direction until you get there.

- You may have to take a few unexpected detours along the way, but if you **stay focused on your goal**, and you keep taking steps toward your goal, eventually you're going to get there.

- **Highly successful people are goal-oriented.** They have a very specific list of goals on which they direct their focus.

- Amazingly, less than 3% of the population actually has a written set of goals. (www.lifeexcellence.com)

- Written goals are far more powerful than "air goals," the ones floating around up there in your head. The goals that are in your head usually stay in your head. That's as far as they go. But write them down, and something magical happens. They become something concrete. Now take those written goals and look at them every day, taking just one small step toward each, every day, and you *will* get there.

- Remember that **wanting and doing are not the same thing.** We all want our students to be successful. But not all teachers actually take the steps necessary to realize that goal. Many just get into a rut and keep doing basically the same thing, year after year after boring year—so they keep getting the same mediocre results.

- Writing your goals is only one step. After writing a goal and getting focused on what it is you really want, then you have to actually start taking steps, small steps—yet consistent steps, toward your goal, every day.

- When it comes to goal setting, one of three things usually happens to make us fail: 1) we set goals but we have no real plan of action, or 2) we set unreasonable goals, so we set ourselves up for failure, or 3) we set realistic goals and have a great plan, but the one minor detail that throws a kink in our best laid plans is that we simply fail to actually put the plan into action!

What you'll accomplish today:

Today, we're going to take three simple steps—and *if* you follow through, you'll accomplish your goals. Here are the steps: 1) You're going to literally define the teacher you want to be—starting tomorrow. 2) Then, based on that definition, you're going to write three realistic goals that you will begin working on tomorrow and write a specific plan for how you'll achieve those goals. 3) The third and final step is that you'll begin taking one action toward those three goals every day. Just one simple action a day—and you'll keep taking small steps until you literally become the teacher you want to be.

Activity

Part 1

If you could be the ideal teacher—the teacher you would like to be–what kinds of characteristics would you possess?

_____

_____

_____

_____

_____

_____

Activity

Part 2

Look back at your list above and place a check next to the top 3 characteristics you would like to possess.

Activity

Part 3

Write those three characteristics you checked and next to each, come up with a goal for how you will develop that particular characteristic in yourself. Turn those three characteristics into three goals that you are committed to accomplishing.

Characteristic 1: _____

Goal: _____

_____

_____

_____

_____

_____

_____

Characteristic 2: _____

Goal: _____

_____

_____

_____

_____

_____

_____

_____

Characteristic 3: _____

Goal: _____

_____

_____

_____

_____

_____

Activity

Part 4

Decide on a time line for accomplishing each goal.

Timeline for Goal #1: _____

Timeline for Goal #2: _____

Timeline for Goal #3: _____

Activity

Part 5

Determine a plan of action by writing at least three things next to each of your goals (above) that you are committed to doing in order to reach each goal.

Assignment

Congratulations! You've got the plan for accomplishing your goals. Now all you have to do is begin to implement your plan of action—tomorrow. Post those three goals somewhere where you'll see them daily, as a constant reminder that you are accomplishing and that you are becoming more effective every single day.

I Had a Plan

I had a plan to make a plan
My New Year's resolution
But since I failed to plan the plan
This still was no solution
The plan did not materialize
I did not follow through
First you have to plan the plan.
Then do what you plan to do!

Annette L. and Elizabeth Breaux

Making the Commitment to Make a Difference

CD 4 Track 1

Your Accomplishments

- You've learned the difference between 1's, 2's, and 3's, along with the importance of being a 3 yourself so that you can help your students to become 3's.

- You've determined the characteristics that make for an effective teacher and have begun to take on those characteristics as your own.

- You're becoming more efficient and effective with your classroom management and discipline plans by implementing consistent routines and procedures in your classroom.

- You're learning to use creative and clever psychology to get students to do what you want them to do.

- You've learned to be more proactive and to defuse potential problems in the classroom.

- You've learned the importance of greeting your students daily at the classroom door.

- You've learned how to minimize "down time" in the classroom.

- You've learned how to better control your actions and reactions with your students.

- You've learned how to maintain your composure even in the toughest situations.

- You've learned how to plan lessons more effectively, relating every lesson to the real life experiences of your students.

- You've learned the importance of maintaining your professionalism at all costs.

- You've learned the importance of your influence.

- And most importantly, you've literally defined the teacher you want to become, and you now have a written plan for accomplishing your goals.

There's only one thing that can stop you now from reaching maximum teaching success, and that's you. But considering the fact that you've stayed the course for the last 10 days, you've got what it takes! In fact, I challenge you to find any school district that would *not* jump at the opportunity to hire a teacher who consistently implements all we've implemented in the last 10 days. The fact is that the majority of teachers in our classrooms do *not* consistently implement all we've implemented in this training. Therefore, you've got a head start on reaching maximum success in the classroom.

Adding to Your Bag of Tricks

- The **"board work"** trick: We all know that students at all age levels love to go to the board. But think about what happens when one student is at the board, or maybe two or three students are at the board. What are the other students typically doing? Not paying attention, right? Well, here's a trick that works like a charm:

  When you send one student to the board, let's say to work on a math problem, have all the other students look at their own problems and put their thumbs up. As long as the student's work at the board agrees with what they have on their papers, their thumbs should stay up. But if the student's work at the board begins to disagree with what they have on their own papers, they put their thumbs down. The student at the board may look back at his classmates as often as he likes, and if he sees lots of thumbs down, he can then check his own work and change it if necessary. This "trick" holds all students accountable while one student is at the board, and it keeps them all on task. It's simple, and it works beautifully! Try it!

- The **"healthy competition"** trick: All you do is divide your class into two teams, and the two teams compete against each other for one grading period. At the end of the grading period, the winning team gets a party and the team with "not quite enough points to win" actually throws the party for them! And of course the psychology behind that one is that everyone gets to attend the party, but the party is planned and hosted by the other team. During the competition, teams earn points for just about anything from behavior, to achievement, to turning in homework, to just about anything you can imagine.

Activity

Think of your one favorite trick—one thing that works well for you with your students regarding behavior or academic achievement or something that fosters understanding of a concept, etc. Write about your favorite trick from your "bag of tricks" here.

_____

_____

_____

_____

_____

_____

_____

_____

_____

_____

_____

_____

_____

_____

_____

_____

_____

_____

_____

_____

Assignment

Share your "trick" with ten teachers. And ask each of the 10 to share their most successful trick with you. You will immediately add 10 more tricks to your bag. Try them out. Some will work and some may not, but you're sure to find a few new tricks to add to your bag.

List the 10 new tricks you've acquired here:

_____

_____

_____

_____

_____

_____

_____

_____

_____

_____

_____

_____

_____

_____

_____

_____

_____

_____

_____

_____

Behind the Mask

If you could see inside of me, then surely you would
know

That beneath my bad behavior is a kid who needs you
so

I need to feel your love for me—I need your caring
smile

I need to be important each day, if only for a while

I need for all your wisdom to pour out onto me

It might not sink in right away—but one day it will,
you'll see

I need a lot of patience, I need a calming voice

I need someone to show me how to make a better
choice

I know it won't be easy—I'll push and test you often

But surely, teacher, you must know that hard hearts
can be softened.

So see me as your challenge, your calling, and your
task

And search until you've found the good that's hidden
behind the mask.

Annette L. Breaux

Conclusion

Remember that your ongoing assignment is to continue to implement what you've learned over the last 10 days every day that you teach–because these 10 days were only the beginning of the rest of your teaching career.

Whether you've been teaching 30 days or 30 years, it's never too late to start over, or, at the very least, to make some positive changes in your teaching. And whenever you need a little inspiration or a little reminder or refresher, simply return to the CDs. Each time you listen to them, you'll become more effective in your teaching. And as your effectiveness increases, your students' achievement will rise.

Finally, don't ever forget that the impression you make on your students today will stay with them for the rest of their lives. They truly do carry us in their hearts forever. And none of us, **none** of us, will ever fully realize the magnitude of our influence as teachers.

It has been my absolute pleasure, honor, and privilege to spend these last 10 days with you. And it is my sincere wish that by applying the simple techniques and strategies we've discussed over the past 10 days, you will reap every reward that teaching has to offer. But, most importantly, it is my sincere wish that your students will be the deserving beneficiaries of a teacher, YOU, who cares, who continues to learn and grow, and who truly believes that every child, yes every child, can succeed!

Now go back to your classrooms and **make a difference!**

Annette L. Breaux

Important Reminder

Don't forget to listen to the bonus session (Disc 4, Track 2) entitled "Achieving Financial Independence on a Teacher's Salary!"

10 Days to Maximum Teaching Success

"A wonderful training that I would recommend for new teachers and veterans alike!"

—Todd Whitaker

10 Days to Maximum Teaching Success is an exciting, innovative approach to staff development, mentoring, and new teacher induction . . . **on AUDIO CDs!**

- Ten highly interactive audio sessions on four CDs that train teachers to maximize their effectiveness.

- Teachers implement daily assignments, work through over 50 activities, and track daily progress in their **Personal Achievement Logs (PAL)**.

- With a special BONUS SESSION—**Achieving Financial Independence on a Teacher's Salary**.

Each session lasts about 20 minutes. Teachers track their progress and complete interactive assignments in their **Personal Achievement Log (PAL)**.

"My faculty LOVED this training, and they're all more effective because of it. Truly a unique, innovative, and effective way to train teachers."

—Noelee Brooks, Principal

10 Days to Maximum Teaching Success
$299.95 plus $13.00 for shipping and handling.
Includes—

- 4 audio CDs
- Instruction booklet
- 10 **PAL**s.

Need extra copies of the PAL? See next page.
See page 64 for more books by Annette Breaux.

Need extra copies of the PAL?

☐ Individual copies cost $8.95 each plus $3.50 for shipping and handling.

☐ Order a **PAL 6-Pack!** Buy 5 copies of the **PAL**, get one FREE! 6 **PAL**s for $44.75 plus $10 for shipping and handling.

☐ Order 100 copies of the **PAL** at $6.95 each (a $200 savings) plus $46 for shipping and handling.

☐ **10 Days to Maximum Teaching Success**—$299.95 plus $13.00 for shipping and handling.

Ship to: _____
          Name

_____
School

_____
Address

_____
City   State   Zip

_____
Phone   Your title

Bill to: _____
          Name

_____
School

_____
Address

_____
City   State   Zip

_____
Phone   Your title

Subtotal (books)   _____

Shipping and Handling   _____

Total   _____

Method of Payment (choose one):

☐ Check (enclosed)   ☐ Credit Card   ☐ Purchase Order

_____   _____
Credit card # (Visa, Master Card, Discover) or PO #   Expiration Date

Eye On Education
6 Depot Way West, Larchmont, N.Y. 10538
(914) 833–0551 Phone (914) 833–0761 Fax
www.eyeoneducation.com

101 "Answers" for New Teachers
& Their Mentors:
Effective Teaching Tips for Daily Classroom Use
Annette L. Breaux

"There is no one I recommend more highly than Annette Breaux."

Harry K. Wong, author
The First Days of School

101 "Answers" for New Teachers & Their Mentors: Effective Teaching Tips for Daily Classroom Use generates instant impact on teaching and learning. Organized so new teachers can read it by themselves, it can also be studied collaboratively with veteran teachers who have been selected to mentor them.

This book—

- offers common sense strategies for any teacher seeking to be more effective.
- supports and sustains master classroom teachers who need help mastering their roles as mentors.
- stimulates and organizes interactive sessions between new teachers and their mentors.

Contents

- Classroom Management
- Planning
- Instruction
- Professionalism, Attitudes, and Behaviors of Effective Teachers
- Motivation and Rapport
- A Teacher's Influence

2003, 180 pp. paperback 1-930556-48-9
$29.95 plus shipping and handling

Order form on page 67

REAL Teachers,
REAL Challenges, REAL Solutions:
25 Ways to Handle the Challenges of the Classroom Effectively

Annette L. Breaux and Elizabeth Breaux

This book is ideal for high-interest staff development workshops or new teacher induction programs. It helps new teachers—and experienced ones—find solutions to common classroom challenges. It presents 25 real scenarios along with "What's Effective," "What's NOT Effective," and "Bottom Line" strategies for handling the most common teacher challenges.

This book shows teachers how to:

- get students to do what you want them to do.
- deal with disrespectful student behaviors and handle "I don't care" attitudes.
- deal with parents and difficult coworkers.
- solve other common teaching challenges.

REAL Teachers, REAL Challenges, REAL Solutions: 25 Ways to Handle the Challenges of the Classroom Effectively is for:

- new teachers who need common-sense answers to common teaching challenges.
- experienced teachers who seek to become even more effective.

2003, 120 pp. paperback 1-930556-64-0
$24.95 plus shipping and handling

Order form on page 67

The Poetry of Annette Breaux:
Poetically Speaking:
25 Tips and Poems for Teachers
No Adults Allowed:
35 Lessons and Poems for Teachers and Students

Finally, Annette Breaux's poems, tips, and lessons in one collection!

If you've been fortunate to attend one of Annette's speeches or have read her books, you know her heartwarming poetry is accompanied by profound lessons for teachers and students. This book is the long-awaited collection of her poems.

Perfect for new teachers, veteran teachers, administrators, and staff developers, this book offers a creative way to improve teaching and learning.

If you have not yet experienced Annette Breaux's poetry, you're in for a real treat!

The Poetry of Annette Breaux is really two books in one:
Poetically Speaking—25 Tips and Poems for Teachers
No Adults Allowed—35 Lessons and Poems for Teachers and Students

2004, 128 pp. paperback 1-930556-92-6
$19.95 plus shipping and handling

Order form on page 67

To order Annette Breaux's other books—

☐ *101 Answers for New Teachers and Their Mentors: Effective Teaching Tips for Daily Classrooom Use.* Breaux. 2003. 176 pp. paperback 1-930556-48-9. $29.95 plus shipping and handling.

☐ *REAL Teachers, REAL Challenges, REAL Solutions: 25 Ways to Handle the Challenges of the Classroom Effectively.* Breaux and Breaux. 2003. 120 pp. paperback 1-930556-64-0 $24.95 plus shipping and handling.

☐ *The Poetry of Annette Breaux.* 2004. 128 pp. paperback 1-930556-92-6. $19.95 plus shipping and handling.

- Order copies as "welcome" gifts for all of your **new** teachers
- Order copies as holiday gifts for **all** of your teachers
- Assign them as required reading in new teacher induction programs
- Assign them in book study groups with experienced teachers

Discounts available on multiple copy purchases—

10–24 copies = 5% Discount   25–74 copies = 10% Discount
75–99 copies = 15% Discount   100+ copies = 20% Discount
(plus shipping and handling. Feel free to call for more information.)

Note: These discounts apply to orders of individual titles and do not apply to combinations of more than one title.

Fill in your address on the other side.

6 Depot Way West
Larchmont, NY 10538
Phone (914) 833-0551   FAX (914) 833-0761
www.eyeoneducation.com

Order Form

Please place your check and/or purchase order with this form in an envelope and mail to *Eye On Education.* If you are not satisfied with any book, simply return it within 30 days in saleable condition for full credit or refund.

Ship to: _____
           Name

_____
School

_____
Address

_____
City   State   Zip

_____
Phone   Your title

Bill to: _____
           Name

_____
School

_____
Address

_____
City   State   Zip

_____
Phone   Your title

Subtotal (books)   _____

Shipping and Handling   _____

Total   _____

Method of Payment (choose one):

☐ Check (enclosed)   ☐ Credit Card   ☐ Purchase Order

_____   _____
Credit card # (Visa, Master Card, Discover) or PO #   Expiration Date

6 Depot Way West
Larchmont, N.Y. 10538
(914) 833–0551 Phone (914) 833–0761 Fax
www.eyeoneducation.com